Essentials Only

A Success Guide to Self-Marketing

DUSTIN BAKER

Copyright © 2021 Dustin Baker

All rights reserved.

ISBN:9798596453706

CONTENTS

1 Building a Brand -1

2 Getting Started with E-mail Marketing -16

3 The Power of Social Media -28

4 SEO Basics -42

Consistency is key. The size of your steps doesn't matter, only the direction you are traveling. Keep going, your goal is within reach.

BUILDING A BRAND

The most important step to go big in the field of business is perhaps Building a Brand. However, this task is not at all simple. It takes many key strategies and a lot of patience in order to turn your company into a successful brand. In this book, we will talk about the whole process of how to build a brand and important tips to help you in your journey.

Building a brand is the most effective way to ensure the success of your business in the long run. It should have an impact on the customers which make them trust in the brand which is the key to run businesses successfully long-term. Having a unique and impactful brand identity can make all the difference between a successful and a failed company.

Although the ultimate goal of every business is to make profit, but while building a brand it should not be your primary goal. People won't buy from you because your brand makes profit, they will buy from you because they trust you, because you have made an emotional connection with your customers through the whole process of building your brand. It all comes down to 3 questions.

What? How? Why?

You need to tell the people exactly what you are doing with the business. Be very clear and simple towards this message. Next, how are you doing it? What necessary steps are needed to be taken in order to do what you do. And finally, why are you doing it? It must be conveyed to the people how the services that your brand provides serves towards their needs, which is essential to make a long-term relationship with your customers.

What is Brand Identity?

The Brand identity basically means what the brand represents. It might be merely the name of your brand but it is the identity of the whole company. The products of the company, the way it communicates with people, values and ethics, logo etc. are all represented by the brand identity. When the world looks at your brand, it should perceive your whole company at a glance. That is why building a brand identity is so important.

Logo

The brand logo is one of the most important choices you need to make while building your brand. It might look simple but the logo says a lot about the brand. This is why making a logo for a brand doesn't come cheap. It takes a good amount of money to hire professionals for designing a brand's logo, because a lot of thought is put into it. The logo is visible on every product the company sells. So it must be something that suits and is in harmony with all their products. It represents your company and demands for the trust of people in it. As soon as we see a trusted logo, we are affected by a sense of trust. Their logo holds such a high standard all because of branding. This is how big brands are well recognized just by their logo.

Design

The design used on business cards, websites, products, logos, etc. all hold utmost importance in building your brand. A unique professional design will leave a permanent positive impression in a customer's mind which will make them purchase again. When you handover your business card to a client, on the first glance they have, the design makes an impact. The website should be designed in such a way which upholds the uniqueness of your products and services to the customers when they visit it. The fonts, the colors, and the styles that are used in the products create an impression. They affect the state of mind of a person.

However it is to be kept in mind that these designs should be consistent throughout everywhere in your company. It basically represents the theme that your company is sticking to. And this theme should represent the products, values, services and the trust that your company provides to its customers.

Audience

Understanding the minds of your customers is one of the key steps towards a successful brand. Different people come with different tastes. You cannot target people with a specific mentality. That leaves you with fewer audiences. The key is to target different people with their different needs. In that way, you gain the trust and love from everyone. Various surveys and market research is required to get an idea about target audiences and their needs. Providing exactly what people are looking for is the best way to build your brand. Market survey can reveal interesting results. You might see increasing demand of something in the market which is not exactly provided by any other company. This is your window of opportunity. Take such opportunities for quick growth in the market even if it means deviating a little from the usual products and services you provide. But remember, too much deviance can give wrong impression to the people.

Competition

You are not the only person who is running a business on the market. There are a lot of other companies who are selling their vast range of products to the people. Staying ahead of your competition and making your company stand out in the market is the ultimate goal of branding. When people want to buy something they would choose your product instead of similar products provided by so many other companies. Understanding and staying up to date with the products and services provided by your competitor companies and taking necessary steps in order to convince people to choose you instead, a necessary and crucial step for building your brand. And people learn more the more they compete. By extensively researching your competition, you might just learn the thing they are lacking and use it in your advantage for quick growth.

Mission

Your brand's mission should be very clear and transparent to your customers. This gives your business a strong and bold personality which is very essential towards the growth of your brand. Sharing your noble visions and goals always lay a positive impact on the minds of people that help you in the long run.

SWOT Analysis

SWOT Analysis is a very useful methodology that is used in the process of building a brand. It goes as:

Strengths: The key aspects of your business that give you a upper hand in the market place amongst your competitors.

Weaknesses: The aspects of your business on which you can improve upon to make it stay ahead of your competition.

Opportunities: New products and services that your business might provide and has a strong probability to grow upon.

Threats: Different aspects of the environment and the business that cause hindrance to the company.

Advertisement

The best way to popularize your brand and make it known among people is by using different form of advertisements. From posters, to TV commercials to the modern day social media posts, advertisement is a powerful tool to make your brand well known to the people.

Posters

Let us start from the traditional method of paper posters. While making it, it should be kept in mind that your brand should leave an impression on the minds of people through it. The graphic designing and the theme discussed above should be in harmony with the message it is trying to convey to the people. Making an emotional connection with customers is always important. The images used in the poster should be eye catching which will make people notice it amid their daily life. The description should be interesting enough for people to read until the last word and it should clearly convey the message as well. Using color overlays and bullet points is a great way to keep it short and interesting. Lastly, it should be creative and unique.

TV Commercial

TV commercials are probably the most effective way to reach out to people. Because who doesn't watch TV right? Making a TV commercial is more challenging compared to posters since a lot more resources are drained in order to make it and run it. Depending on the channels where you run your ad, your bill could get ridiculously high. So every second counts. The goal is to make an impact on the people watching TV which makes them try out your products and services and turn into regular customers. The commercial video should be simple enough to make people understand about your brand, the products and services you provide, and why it is better than your competitor companies. But it should not be boring which will make people look away whenever your commercial is running. Hiring celebrities to feature in your commercial is a popular way to reach people, although expensive. Video choreography, VFX, animations, dialogues, everything is important while creating a commercial. People are greatly influenced by motivational and humorous commercials. It always leaves a positive and curious impression in their minds. Because we know, the most important thing is to make that emotional connection with your target audience in order to be recognized and grow among the masses.

Social Media

Social Media is the modern day tool of advertisement. In the age of internet and smartphones, we know how much a person spends their time around social media. So, creating an official Facebook page with your brand's name and making a verified twitter account of the same is very important. Social media is regarded to be the most powerful tool in marketing now a day. Separate educational degrees are provided on "Social media marketing". A huge number of people are working in this field, promoting businesses on social media. Being in this modern day market, using social media to build your brand is a must. Making your brand reach more people is basically making your page reach more. You have to be very active with your page in order to reach more people. The 'share' option is a very powerful tool which can make your audience do your work to reach more people. Following social media trends, making eye catching posts will make people share your posts in their own social media which will further attract more people and the cycle repeats. That is why being daily active in your page is so important. Apart from Facebook, twitter, Instagram, using video streaming websites to make people watch your advertisements is also very popular and effective. Advertisements are even shown in many apps in your smartphone. That's the power of modern day technology. There are also a number of companies who can promote your brand by sending bulk email addresses by their email scrapping methods, thus reaching a huge number of people.

Sponsorships

Lastly, we will talk about advertisement through sponsorships. Sponsoring events, charity causes, trade shows and famous individuals always make you stand out in the market. It makes the emotional bond between the customers and your brand stronger, since it is not a direct form of advertisement. Your brand is paying to support a cause that is important to the people. One of the biggest advantages of sponsorship is that it automatically generates media exposure. It further strengthens the ethics and values of your brand. Sponsoring events and shows make your brand reach more people and VIP from other industries which further enhances connection with the world. Many sponsorship opportunities also let you introduce your products and services to the people around which turn them into potential customers and generates further new leads.

Customer Service

If you are doing business, customers are your upmost priority. The ones who are truly responsible in making your brand a success are none other than customers. This is why feedback, and responding to customer queries and grievances are so important. Your brand should have an active customer care number, email and as the modern day demands, their social media counterparts as well. Using chat bots to answer the FAQs of the customers is a smart way to automate the interaction between the customers and your brand. Being polite and humble while interacting with customers is the key to earn their trust. Your customer service is basically the voice of your brand.

Things to Avoid

- Misleading your customers by giving them false promises or information about your brand's products or services can lead to devastating downfall of your company. Once getting infamous as fake, a brand can almost never recover from such a phase. This is why being honest and truthful to your customer is of utmost importance.

- Do not promote any kind of racism or sexism through your brand's advertisements. Make sure no tinge to racism or sexism is being portrayed through your posts.
- Never leave a customer angry. Customer grievances should not be taken lightly. One angry customer can influence a lot others to walk the same path. Some even spread false rumors about the brand that upset them.
- Never copy your competition. Nobody likes an imposter copy in the market. If you copy products or services from other companies just because they are popular, you will always live in their shadows and your brand will not become a success. Improving upon business ideas is one thing and completely copying business ideas is another. Avoid the later.
- Never be obsessed with favourites. It doesn't matter how much money you made by selling a product to the people. The market and its demands change from time to time. Be dynamic enough to adapt to those demands and improvise accordingly so that you never get left out in the competition. Providing people with exactly what they want is the key to a successful brand.

Work Force

Hiring efficient and loyal employees should be your all time goal while building your brand. Your employees should share the same vision and goals as your brand in order for it to make a success. All the above said work cannot be done without them. Loyalty is very important in the brand business. Your work force will be exposed to confidential information which is a key to your brand's success and makes it stand out in the market. Such information could be sold easily for a lucrative amount to the competitors. This is why you always need to monitor the affairs of your brand and make sure the ethics and values, which your brand is based upon is maintained. Always try to keep your employees happy and maintain a toxicity-free work environment. Hiring interns is always a profitable way to boost your business. Keep an eye out for efficient students who will do great work for you for a considerably lower amount of money, and they get work experience in return. You should always maintain a bold and imperative attitude with your employees while being humble at the same time. Never forget, they are the building blocks of your brand.

Brand's Story

People love inspiration. Sharing your brand's story, on how you decided to start it from scratch, how you were inspired, the early day struggles, and how it ultimately became what it is today motivates a lot of people. Such motivation not only lays a positive impact on the society, but does its magic of attracting more customers and creating that emotional bond. This is also a great way to attract efficient and loyal employees who share commons goals and visions. Because of humble beginnings, a lot of people prefer to work with such a company because it makes them feel safe and comfortable. And also they try to give it their best in order to grow along with the company.

As I have said before, building your brand is not an easy task. But you always need to keep your heads up. Initially it comes with a lot of investment with minimum profit which demotivates a lot of businessmen who have started to build their brand. But it should not be a cause for you to stop from achieving what you were set out to achieve. The competition is high, but the market is vast as well. There will be ups and downs in this journey. Learn to take lessons from the times when you are down in order to make it up the next time and move on. Always make sure to highlight the uniqueness of your brand. This is how big brands make it to the top. They are unique, they listen to what people need, they are flexible with their services and that's how they maintain their constant grip on the marketplace.

Branding can do wonderful things towards your business. It won't be another nameless and faceless organization that people can trust. People will talk about it among themselves; even inspire others to buy from you. You keep getting customers coming back for more, with even new ones. Branding allows you to increase the prices of your products without losing customers. It is something the power of your brand has granted you. The trust and the premium feeling that people get from your brand are not lost easily. It stays and makes you grow even more multiplying your initial investments to huge numbers and turning it into profit.

GETTING STARTED WITH E-MAIL MARKETING

E-mail marketing has been down-played over the years with social media platforms taking the spotlight. Don't let this fool you. E-mail marketing is still known as the most effective and direct way to connect with potential consumers.

Making e-mail marketing a top contender on your priority list would be a wise investment. One of the main advantages is that you own your e-mail list. This can't be said for social media platforms that can be terminated or otherwise blocked from using. All those contacts. Gone.

Studies have also shown that sales compared between e-mail marketing and social media marketing differ with e-mail marketing coming out on top with two-thirds of the revenue.

So, what is e-mail marketing? E-mail marketing is the process of collecting personal information, in this case names and e-mail addresses, that show an interest in your product or service. These e-mail addresses are then used to send e-mail advertisements, information and links to your website. This efficiently puts your product or service in front of the right people and can increase traffic and sales exponentially.

So, I've caught your attention and you're ready to learn more. It's got to be complicated right? Wrong. Like most things in life, e-mail marketing is only as complicated as you make it.

What You Will Learn

In this book you will learn the basics of e-mail marketing. You will learn what an e-mail list is, why it is so important, and why it is often referred to as your "money maker". You will learn what lead magnets are and how to properly use and write them. You will learn how to format both lead magnets and e-mails. We will also touch base on e-mail automation and how it works as well as landing pages and the important role they can play in e-mail marketing.

The skills in this book are just the basics, the *key* basics to get you rolling using email marketing in hours, not days or weeks.

You will learn how to apply those skills and truly benefit from e-mail marketing. Learn all you can and apply what you have learned. The only direction from here is up!

Getting Started

While some subscription software programs make your life a little easier, they are not necessary to get started with e-mail marketing but highly recommended. Most come with a free trial and are fairly inexpensive. A simple online search will provide you with multiple choices. Read reviews and research what each one offers before making a decision. This will provide you with the best software to fit your individual needs.

You can take a more "old school" approach but keep in mind it requires a lot of leg-work and time. Whichever way you choose, the first step is simply getting started.

The first objective to focus on is your e-mail list.

E-mail List

If you are starting with a software program, most of the work has been done for you. Once you get the program set up for your business, you are provided with e-mail addresses or leads. These will be specific for your business and area.

If starting without a program, you will have to hunt these down one at a time searching for the best fit company e-mails. A huge downfall with this, chances of ending up in a spam folder are quite good. You can also buy leads but there is no way of knowing if they are "dead" leads that are going to be a waste of time. I do not recommend buying leads.

Lead Magnets

A lead magnet is something you are offering for free in exchange for a "lead" or e-mail address. Most commonly these are things that are either cheap or free to create. The reader subscribes to get the free gift and by doing so, you now have their name and e-mail address. Now you just turned a reader into a potential lead.

Digital files that are most often used include:

-eBooks

-free consultation

-free quote/estimate

-samples

-coupons

The goal here is to give something that will give the consumer the feeling of value. If you control emotions, you control sales.

Lead Magnet Creation

Copywriting skills come in handy here but are not required. You just have to be creative. This can also be outsourced to a freelance writer if preferred. You are trying to sale something without seeming pushy. Be unique and creative. Just don't go overboard. The goal is to obtain personal information. Be sure to include any or all of the following in your subscription form:

-Name

-E-mail address

-Phone

-Company name

-Social media links

In this case the more information the better but be careful. Don't make your form so long to fill out that no one takes the time to complete it. Find a balance. Try different variations and review. See what works for your particular business. Keep good records for later reference. This will save time in the long run. Especially if you decide to diversify or when creating new lead magnets in the future.

Your headline is crucial. If the reader doesn't get past the headline, you didn't even get a chance getting that lead let alone a sale. Be clear and direct.

Your description should be short and not go into too much detail. Make the format easy to read. Add spacing or bullets. Break up big groups of words that may turn the reader off to finishing the lead magnet therefore the rest of the process.

Add graphics and gifs for extra pizazz. Colors and movement are eye catching. Use this to your advantage here. This is also a good way to optimize your subscribe button. Make it appealing. Make them want to click it. Make it irresistible.

Some good tips for making a lead magnet:

-Short-winded

-Provides Improvement

-Accessible now

-Eye catching

You don't want your lead magnets full of dull content or "fluff". After reading a few lines the reader will get bored or impatient and only skim the content. This could cost you a good lead.

Providing improvement is crucial. If the readers do not gain anything, why would they waste their time? If this happens, the chances of them opening another e-mail from you are slim to none. This goes back to adding value. Provide a skill or tool that will consistently improve their knowledge and skillset. They will keep coming back for more.

Let's face it, people are impatient. If you offer something that isn't available until a later date, more than likely that offer will be ignored entirely. Make sure whatever you offer out is accessible now.

Consumers get a sense of satisfaction receiving things that are beneficial to them. This is especially true with something that is free. Again, if you control emotions, you control sales.

Now that you have made your lead magnet or opt in form, as it is commonly referred to, it's time to put it on your website. Utilize creative ways to do this as well. Try the header, footer or sidebar for starters. Floating button? Let your creative juices flow!

Sending E-mails

Now that you have your list of leads, it's time to create your e-mail. When creating, pay close attention to the content. Know your audience. Again, If the reader has a pleasant experience with one of your e-mails, they are more likely to open and read future e-mail they receive from you.

Make sure your content contains value. Don't send e-mails just to send them thinking more e-mails automatically means more consumers. It simply doesn't work that way.

Give yourself some patience here and play around with the content until you see what works. Graphics and gifs can be utilized here as well. After all, you're trying to catch their attention and keep it. Change format or tone and evaluate again. Trial and error lead to great results as long as the lessons are learned and applied.

Landing Pages

Landing pages are another helpful marketing tool. They are basically just single-page websites. While not all landing pages play into e-mail marketing, lead generating landing pages plays a huge role in it. Lead generating landing pages are for obtaining personal information. These type of landing pages usually do not contain graphics or flash. Simple and to the point.

Other types of landing pages include long-form and product descriptions. A long-form landing page is basically an informative article. These landing pages are to inform in detail about a product or service. Usually not written in a "pushy" tone, these landing pages are for learning about a product or service.

Product description landing pages are just that. Descriptions of a product or service. These usually have graphics and are written to entice sales.

Automation

Once you get the process going, you can save yourself a lot of time by using automated e-mails. Much like the lead generation software, there are services that you can subscribe to that will send your e-mails automatically.

You can choose and save different templates you have made and set a schedule of when they go out. Not only can you choose the time but the contacts as well. This will free up more time to tackle other tasks. This is an excellent way to improve efficiency.

When creating automatic e-mails, if you haven't already, play into each group of potential consumers individually. Target by location or age group and write your e-mails accordingly. This will save you time later when designating what goes where. If you have multiple templates for each group pre-made, it's as simple as dividing them up into their own groups instead of trying to keep up with trends and always adding countless new e-mail templates.

Pro Tips

-When creating your e-mail list, take advantage of social media. This will help give you and your product or service more exposure to potential leads. Add a link to your landing page. Be sure to use the proper hashtags to connect with the proper audience. You would be surprised how many leads that this can generate.

-Blogging is becoming more and more popular as the days roll by. Take advantage of that. Add a blog to your website if one doesn't already exist. This is another key place you can put a link to your landing page and generate more leads. Blog about your journey in business or about the history and current status of your industry. An advantage here is that the people following your blog will already be the right audience due to your blogging topic. Be sure to add links to your blog on social media for even more exposure.

-Your e-mail list is your "money-maker". Take care of it. Be sure to always keep it organized. Clean out old contacts that are non-responsive. Allow for easy unsubscribing. Consumers that want to unsubscribe but can't figure out how or that simply don't want to take the time to complete a lengthy process are not a benefit to you anyway. Don't waste your time. Focus on who wants to engage.

-Never under-estimate the power of testing your methods. Test every variation and technique that you try. After testing, test again. Feedback from your actions is pivotal to success. It's near-impossible to learn what works and what doesn't without testing. The importance of this cannot be stressed enough.

-To improve you open rates, send your e-mails during traditional work hours and after lunch breaks. Put the readers' name in the subject line for added personalization. This gives the e-mail the appearance that it is more important and the reader needs to open it and find out what it is.

Put These Skills to Action

The hardest part of taking on any new task is simply getting started. Getting that motivation to begin. I can assure you, that is the hardest part of getting started with e-mail marketing. Take your time and go through this one step at a time. I think you will quickly learn that e-mail marketing isn't as daunting as it seems and the rewards can be plentiful!

This book was created to be a basic guide to get started with e-mail marketing. E-mail marketing is a huge topic and there is tons more to learn. While you can effectively engage and benefit from only following the steps in this book, don't stop there! Learn as much as you can. Knowledge is power. Power that no one can take away from you. Embrace it. Use it. Grow and excel!

THE POWER OF SOCIAL MEDIA

In the beginning, people used social media to connect. But over time, they started to use and trust social media more and more. Billions of people of all ages interact with each other directly via social media and in various communities. The response, brands came to realize they had to be more relatable with their customers and the community. All this shows us the growing influence of social networks in marketing.

Social media has given consumers power and control, which took advantage of well-known brands and large corporations. Now, everyone has the same opportunity to reach a specific audience. Business owners, top-level executives, and marketers have realized that social media can make or break their business. After analyzing their data to know their target audience, they're creating strategies to plug their products and services to the public on social media. And CRM can help you to get better results.

Today more than ever, businesses recognize the immense opportunities of having a trusted online presence. No one can deny the powerful importance of Social Media marketing. If used wisely, Social Media is a powerful business tool. For several years, Social Media Marketing has been shown to be the fastest-growing marketing trend with 9 out of 10 companies reporting employing some type of social media marketing campaign.

Importance of Social Media in Marketing

When we talk about Digital Marketing today, many people think directly about social networks. These communication channels are a recurring theme in famous publications, the subject of various conferences, and the subject of countless books. At the end, what are the characteristics of social networks, and why are they important for Marketing?

Our traditional media are TV, radio, newspaper, magazines, and billboards. Something in common in all of these? They are one-way media, one side speaks and the other only listens. With Twitter, Facebook, YouTube, blogs and so many other sites, we achieve quite broad means of communication and with a great difference from traditional media: everyone has the right to point out (as content producers) and to possess a voice (as consumers). Therefore, social networks are everyone's means of communication for everything.

People are more committed to having space and constant interactions and the message gains more credibility since the person speaking is an acquaintance whom we trust. It is not like the advertising in which the company is interested in making you buy their product. On social media, you can see someone making a recommendation, usually without any commitment to the company. It's word of mouth in expanded proportions.

A quick visit on Twitter, for example, it's easy to see people comment on brands and products. The decision to be on social media is independent of the company: people decide whether to talk about it. And if they speak, they are the ones who decide whether to speak well or poorly of the company.

However, a company that thinks about results in Digital Marketing must optimize its presence on the Internet. The role of Marketing is to realize and serve the market. Social media enhances the ability of any business to better understand the needs of its customers.

To better understand the market, the company must monitor what is said about it, its products, and its competitors. You must extend your communication channels to social networks, allowing the user himself to get in touch and talk more about his needs.

Having a great product is important in serving the market. However, you can also serve it by providing useful content for the user, through your company's profile on social networks. In this way, you can be providing the ammunition users need to spread your message.

In this book, we will cover 15 of the biggest reasons why the power of social media in marketing is important to your business.

Increase in Traffic

The first and not so obvious benefit of social media is that it helps increase your website traffic. By sharing your content on social media, you are giving users a reason to click on your website. On your social media account, the more quality content you share, the more inbound traffic you'll generate while also creating conversion opportunities.

Many people, and also businesses, make the mistake of simply posting to social media channels, leaving their website abandoned, if they have one at all. This is a horrible mistake. Why? First of all, you must understand that "your channel" of social networks is NOT yours. You, as a user, have access to use it. Even though it is "free", you are not the owner. The correct way to do this is first and foremost to create high-quality content on your website and then share it on social media platforms. In this way, you will benefit from the power of this traffic and if people like your content, they will not only wait for you to publish it on your channel, but they will come back for more quality content on your website. Also, it is on your website that you have full control, not on social media channels. And something very essential is that you make sales on your website, you receive money on your website, not on social networks. That is why your website should be the centrist of your business on the Internet.

It's good to remember that aside from traffic, the content sharing rate on social media also increases domain authority for content that was shared, resulting in a higher position or ranking in search engines. A rule of thumb is that the first thing you should do is think about the importance of a good domain.

Improved Brand Recognition

Using social media allows your customers to link and interact with your company on a more personal level. If you already have an established brand, social media could be an opportunity to further develop your brand and give your business a voice.

When your company publishes regularly on social media platforms, this allows it to interact with customers in a more familiar way. This constant interaction creates an image of credibility and a desire to hear what customers have to say. Once customers are familiar with your brand, they are more likely to recommend your brand to friends and family, increasing the reach of your brand.

Obtain Valuable Information from the Audience

The nature of social media allows these platforms to collect vast amounts of data about each individual user. As users of social networks, we provide information about what our favorite hobbies, our jobs, gender, age, location, and much more. All of our activity on social media, including shares, likes, retweets; provides information about ourselves and our feelings towards various brands.

Most companies with a successful social media presence use some form of social listening, which are analytics tools that constantly collect useful customer data and track conversations about target brands or topics. Using social listening tools allows us to collect relevant data on audiences to establish results-based campaigns.

Fast Customer Service and Satisfaction

One of the biggest benefits of having the services of a social media marketer is that your business almost immediately gets a voice online, not just your website. Creating a voice for your company is vital to enhance the general image of the brand. Customers appreciate the fact that when they post comments on your page, they receive a human response rather than a computerized message. A brand that values its customers takes the time to write a personal message, which is naturally perceived in a positive way. The traditional way to complain was to send emails with your dissatisfaction regarding a product or service. Times have changed and customers have changed too. We have moved on from our heavily worded letters to sending very hasty and aggressive tweets to companies. Over 67% of consumers now go to social media for customer service, which means the need for customer service on social media is essential. By using response automation or even real humans (which is best) to answer inquiries on social media, companies can ensure that their customers receive prompt service.

Low Marketing Costs

Compared to conventional marketing, Social Media Marketing does not require a large number of monetary resources. As the business landscape continues to evolve, traditional marketing methods begin to terminate in favor of less resource-intensive methods. Therefore, using social media to market products and services is an efficient way to reduce operating costs for businesses

If you decide to use paid advertising on social media, always start small to see what to expect. Being economical is important as it helps you obtain a higher return on investment and have a larger budget for other commercial and marketing payments. By just investing a little money and time, you can significantly increase your conversion rates and, finally, get a return on investment on the money you invested and then scale to other levels.

Scope of the target audience

Many people think that having an effective social media presence is simply having a large following. While this is important, it is not the only way to reach your audience on social media, let alone the smartest way. Something very important that you should know is that the reach of followers on social networks has been decreasing.

On Facebook, for example, by 2012, the reach was 16%. That means that if a person or company had 100 fans, or people who like their Facebook page, and that person made a publication, it would reach about 16 people, not 100. For the year 2018, that percentage dropped to almost 7%. This is simply concerning.

Potential to Convert Followers into Customers

Social media is the superior way to interact with customers. The more you communicate and interact with your audience, the more chances you've got of conversion. Establish a two-way communication with your target audience so that their wishes are known and their interest is easily attended to. In addition, communication and service with customers is one of the ways to attract their attention and convey your brand message to them.

Therefore, your brand will reach more audience in real terms and will establish itself without problems. A potential customer can learn a lot about a company by seeing how agile their activity is on social media. As human nature dictates: we want to go where our friends like to go. If a brand can turn a follower into a customer through social media, that customer generally becomes a more loyal fan. rare statistics that 53% of Americans who follow brands on social media are more faithful to those brands. With the increased brand visibility that comes with social media advertising, more potential customers will visit your website and the chances of conversion increase. With a well-prepared social media advertising plan, a business can improve its sales and profits. By the way, in marketing jargon, the word " leads " means prospect or potential customer.

Competition Analysis

Social media is the best way to analyze your competition.
They allow you to see what your competition is doing, and they can see you too. It's a fair deal for everyone. You can see how they interact with their audience, the frequency of posts, the kind of content they produce or share, etc. Social monitoring is a great way to measure your industry and see how you stand out from your competition. In other words, you can see what your competition is doing, do it too, and even improve it.

Improve Loyalty

For a company to stay afloat, it needs a loyal customer base. New customers are a happy addition, but without loyal ones, conversion rates would be somewhere between sad and non-existent. Social media advertising creates an open service platform where customers can express their views and feelings about the services and products offered.

By listening to consumer feedback, customer satisfaction levels increase exponentially and, along with them, build loyalty to your brand.

When you have a presence on social media, you make it easier for your customers to seek out and connect with you. By connecting you with your customers through social media, you're more likely to increment customer retention and customer loyalty. Developing a loyal customer base is one of the primary goals of almost any business. Customer satisfaction and brand fidelity often go hand in hand.

It is essential that you engage with your customers and begin to develop a bond with them. Social media is not limited to introducing your product; They are also a vital platform for promotional campaigns. A customer sees these platforms as service channels where they can communicate directly with the company.

Market Knowledge

One of the best ways to meet the needs and wants of your customers instead of communicating directly with them is market knowledge. It is also considered to be one of the most important advantages of social media. By looking at the activities on your profile, you can see the interest and opinions of customers that you would not otherwise know if you had no presence to them. As a complementary research tool, social media can help you gain insight and insight into your industry. Once you have a large following, you can use additional tools to examine other demographics of your consumers.

Brand Authority

It doesn't matter if you are a starting entrepreneur or a large company, you need to build authority with your brand.

When customers see your business transmission on social media, especially by responding to their query and posting original content, you help them build a positive image in their minds. Interacting regularly with your customers shows that you and your company care about them. Once you have a few satisfied customers expressing their positive shopping experience, you can let genuine customers who appreciate your product or service advertise for you.

Better Positioning in Search Engines

The more people who talk about your business on social media, as well as recommending, following and liking, the better your search ranking will be. Word of mouth is still relevant. Who do people believe most: the reviews of your products on your website or the people you know? It's the latter, so you shouldn't underestimate the power of word of mouth. Keep your customers happy and satisfied, and they will become advocates for your brand by telling their friends, family, and acquaintances.

If your company has a list on social networks, it is most likely that you will appear among the main search results of a related product or service, which will generate greater visibility. Search engine optimization tools are another attractive option due to their ability to drive more traffic to company websites and achieve higher rankings on them.

Instant Content Distribution

In a world where people want instant gratification, the need to provide customers with instant content and marketing has become very important. Social media channels make it easy to post information and reach many people in a short time.

Real Time Feedback

One of the most useful benefits that the Social Media Marketing service offers is real-time feedback. Your customers can ask about almost any topic related to your business or service and will receive a quick response from the marketing team. This sends them a message of confidence.

Due to this, companies can incorporate the "human factor", allowing a more natural relationship with consumers. Social media can act as the free-and-easy medium between a brand and its audience to provide information, contests, giveaways, and a lot of other things. Of course, time is defined and managed in the channel, but it is a good way to stay in touch with your potential customers, who will eventually become your customers.

Income

The last reason in this book is Income, in other words, making money. Having an effective social media presence allows more users to go through the marketing funnels and end up on a page where they can make a purchase. If your website is well done and converts well, it's safe to say that your sales will increase with the growth of social media.

Pro-Tips

• Social Networks are an incredible and excellent way to attract new customers.

• Marketing in Social Networks has become an extremely important and powerful business tool. The Internet is undoubtedly the main marketing highway in the world. Now more than ever, businesses recognize the immense opportunities that a trusted online presence provides.

• By spending just a few hours a week, more than 91% of marketers said that their social marketing efforts greatly increased their brand visibility and increased the user experience. Without a doubt, having a social media page for your brand will benefit your business and, with regular use, it can also generate a large audience for your business in no time.

• Social media is becoming one of the most important aspects of digital marketing, offering incredible benefits that help reach millions of customers around the world. And if you are not applying this profitable source, you are missing an undreamed marketing opportunity, as it makes it easy to get the word out about your product and goal.

Without a doubt, Social Media Marketing has many benefits for startups and established brands. By regularly updating your social media channels with the right strategies, you will get more traffic, improve your SEO, get better search engine rankings, have a better relationship with your customers, and also develop brand authority.

Chances are, your competition is already working on these strategies, so don't let your competitors take over their customers. The earlier you start, the quicker you will see your business grow.

One of the biggest problems that entrepreneurs face is a lack of time, knowledge, and technical processes to prepare for the many steps a profitable strategy needs to function properly. Yes, it is correct: There is no doubt that you can generate from a modest income online to a high level. It's no secret that many internet marketers cross the 7-figure barrier every year. There are even some who make more than 8 figures a year.

Take the time to create. Don't solely consume. The time is there. You just have to motivate yourself enough to get started. It all goes up from here!

SEO BASICS

Search Engine Optimization (SEO) corresponds to the practices that allow increasing the quantity and quality of visitors who come to a website through organic searches on search engines, such as Google. Understanding how search engines such as Google , Bing or Yahoo work and how to arrange textual or multimedia content to favor indexing is vital to acquire good habits and improve SEO (search engine optimization), it helps to invest the appropriate time and effort , thinking about its advantages to attract the target audience in a more natural way, thanks to the results of their searches and other interactions.

The search engine generates indexes by classifying all the contents that are generated or updated, and it does so in a similar way to how a bookstore or library is organized , taking as reference a series of data such as the title , a summary description , the name of the author , the theme or subject on which the content deals with to classify it, a publication date, its geographical location and more aspects as secondary actors to the previous ones.

What is SEO?

To understand the function of SEO, we first have to know the function of search engines. In the old days, when the modem signal was used, and before Google changed the world, we relied on site directories. So we would jump from one directory to another, looking for the sections that covered our topic, such as travel, computers, food, etc. Then we dedicated ourselves to going from site to site until we found the one that had the information we were looking for.

If you are a little older, you probably remember that this was a tedious process for which you needed patience, time and tenacity to find the right website. With the appearance of search engines such as Yahoo, Google and Ask, their reason for being was to enter "the most suitable website for your search terms." Until today, this is the fundamental principle of any search engine, which is why each search engine has written its own algorithm to determine which website is most relevant for any term used in the search.

In essence, Google, Yahoo, and others try to find the website with the most suitable content for a term. As a consequence, **SEO** is the attempt to make your website more relevant than that of your competition and to be shown among the first in the SERP (Search Engine Results Page).

Why should I be interested in SEO?

Unless everything you touch turns to gold or you have a budget of more than seven figures that allows you to build your brand through mass media advertising, sponsorship of sports teams and public relations, then you depend on the people looking for the right. product or service you offer (keywords and key phrases).

You may have the most creative site in the world, but if you don't appear in the SERP for keywords related to your industry, then you are floating in the abyss of the Internet. Yes, you will be in the middle of Preciados street with the most beautiful store, but without customers.

How do I optimize my website?

Remember that the golden rule of SEO is relevance. Everything you hear about SEO strategies, magic tricks, secret codes, and more, are all ways of telling search engines that you are the most relevant.

Do you remember when in school the teacher would stand in front of the class and ask questions and you got excited raising your hand to answer because she knew the answer while you thought "Teacher, teacher, teacher, choose me"? This is how SEO works! You are trying to attract the attention of the teacher or, in this case, the search engine, because you have the answer. Except you can't raise your hand, jump out of the chair or call the teacher.

Simply put, SEO is the process by which you make your site relevant by sending the right signals to search engines.

What are signals for SEO?

There are two types of signals that keep search engines in check: On-Page signals and off-page signals. There are roughly more than 600 signals that make up the Google and Yahoo algorithms, so there is no way we can list them all without losing your will to keep living, so we will do our best to give you the most important ones.

What are On-Page signs?

These are the messages that your website and content are directly responsible for, which means they are present in the content and encoding of your website so that you can control them directly. These include:

Domain name

Yes, you are reading well. Your domain name should include the keywords. It should have meaning on its own because if not, as a joke, it needs no explanation. This means that before choosing a domain you should think about SEO . If you already have one, then you should follow the tips below:

URL

Your page URL should include your target keywords and specifically the keywords that are targeted by the keyword on each page. This means that if your page is about chocolate ice cream, then your URL must include "chocolate ice cream". You should also take note of the next point, namely "Content structure".

Content structure

The way you group your content gives a good clue to search terms. Using sub-addresses to separate information in a logical way is not only good practice for managing your website, but also a signal for Google, Yahoo, etc. about the content of your site. This is why you should think about SEO before designing your website. Taking the example above, if your site is about food, then you should separate the content into sub-addresses like "ice cream" or "desserts" or other headings. As you can see, the signals are not only about the page but also about the structure of the content on your site.

Navigation keys

The navigation keys do not have to follow the structure of your website and can give search engines more clues about the interconnectedness of the content. You can either follow the content structure and reflect it in your navigation key, or make your navigation help the visitor to find the information more easily. This is a combination of usability and SEO signal that go hand in hand.

Structure of the content on the page

This brings us back to the classroom. Do you remember the basic rules about writing a text and the use of headings, subtitles, paragraphs, etc.? These rules remain in effect on the Internet and on websites, since both Google and other search engines use these signals to map the structure of your content on the page. Titles and subtitles appear in the code as "H1" - "Hx" to show the hierarchy of content. You can also use colors and fonts to give more visual emphasis of this structure to the reader, as well as the search engine.

Meta tags: title

This is an excerpt of the content for a given page. Each page should have a unique title that includes the keywords or key phrases from that page and not the keywords from your website. Remember that it is the specific page and not the website, so you must explain the content in less than 60 characters, which is the limitation of the display of the SERP page.

Meta tags: description

This is the long 160-character version of your content that, once again, should include the page's target keywords (not necessarily your website), but should also engage users as it is visible within the SERP (see black text in SERP image). The description is your "sales pitch," but it should appeal to both visitors and search engines.

Meta tags: keywords

There is a wide debate about how Google considers this aspect because there were abusive practices in the past. In addition to Google, other search engines took notice and this can serve as a guide for the future. In 6 months you won't remember which keywords you are using today! However, we are not suggesting that you fill the page with keywords or key phrases. You should use a keyword a maximum of 5 times per page with the most important at the beginning and the least relevant at the end.

Language code

The language indicated in the *header* of the code indicates to search engines and browsers the language used on a given page. This allows browsers to display the correct characters as well as to provide search engines with the language of your audience. Remember that for a multilingual site, each page must have a different code.

Alt-Text (alternative text)

Remember that Google and other search engines cannot read or decipher images. This implies that no matter how visually rich your website is, in SEO only text counts. In this way, each image must be described in words so that the search engine can understand its relevance and purpose. Whenever possible, target keywords should be used within the description to emphasize their relevance. Alt-Tag is used within HTML code to provide textual information about an image to search engines.

Loading speed

This has become increasingly important since Google also takes "user experience" into account. Pages that take a long time to load are penalized and remain in the lowest positions of the results, so you should avoid heavy images without compression, gimmicky graphics that make the page heavier, and do not fill the page with code.

Responsive Design

This gained importance due to the wide use of smartphones and tablets. This means that your website adapts to the width of the visitor's device screen and displays the content according to those parameters. Again, this is customer service and common sense.

SSL (Secure Socket Layer)

SSL is a security and authentication certificate that you can add to your site. It is generally not needed unless you have an online store and handle financial transactions.

Site Map

There are two types of sitemap. One is a list of pages for search engines, latest update, priority, etc. This is important because it supports the structure of your site and gives the date of the last update of each page. Search engines are passionate about fresh content! The second sitemap is for humans, which includes URLs and a simple site description in case you get lost on the website. This is less important currently, but it is good practice.

Archives Robots

This is text that tells search engines which directories they can scan and index into, which directories to read only (but not index), and which ones are banned. It is also a good idea to emphasize this on each page using Robot Meta Tag per page.

As you may have already realized, on-page SEO starts before your site even sees the light of day. The SEO should start with the selection of the domain name, the structure of the content, structure and URL naming convention. Now you can see why you should start thinking about SEO before buying your domain. If you've already committed to a domain name, then you shouldn't embark on your website design without first turning to people who understand SEO . Your website should have SEO built into the design and not be an afterthought.

What is Off Page SEO?

Off Page SEO is the actions you take outside of your website to send signals to search engines that determines your website content relevance to a given search term also known as Keywords or Key phrases.

What are Off-Page Signals?

Now you are entering the dark art of SEO. Nobody really knows for certain but everyone has an opinion and "thinks" they know the 600+ signals. The key here is about experience and we are sharing here some of the key signals that we have seen impact websites. This is not an exhaustive list of elements and do remember search engines change their algorithm regularly.

PageRank

This is based on the number of links from other websites that are pointing to your website. This is defunct as we see more and more websites with lower Page Ranks beat higher ranked ones in SERP. In March 2016 Google announce it will no longer publish Page Ranks. This is understandable as so many people have tried to game the system by buying or trading links. Google in particular started to penalize sites that it suspects are buying links, so be very wary of buying or trading links even in triangular trade (This is where you put a link to one website, which has a link to a 3rd website that in turn puts a link to your website!).

You should also stay away from Directories and Link Farms as the only thing that helps in SEO is "Relevant Links" from "Relevant Sites" and not sheer numbers. It is of no use having a link from a grocery website if your website is about car hire. So you need links from good quality and trusted websites that have relevant content to your subject. You can stop obsessing about PageRank now and concentrate on getting natural links which means unpaid links from relevant websites to your website.

Domain Age

New domains are always at a disadvantage when it comes to SERP (Search Engine Results Page) performance. Google needs to trust your website. Google's trust is built by a combination of age, number of links from trusted websites, content quality, website performance, ownership, and length of time the domain is paid for (commitment to the web as it is known within the SEO circles).

If the domain has been active, i.e. with an active website and not a holding page, then optimization of this site should be much easier than a brand new domain. However, if the active website is relatively new, then the aging process would have only started from the moment a live website was installed.

Back Links

Firstly what is the difference between Back Links and Links? Well none except Links can be internal or externals links, whilst back links are always links from an external source (another website, social media, etc.) to your website. This means a link from Facebook is a back link just as a link from another website to you is a back link. However, the value of the back link, also referred to as "Link Juice", is based on how highly thought of (or trusted) is the website linking to you and also how relevant they are. The more links you have the better for your website but only if they are from reputable and relevant websites or sources.

Link Juice

The impact of a link on your website is dependent on the originating site's (or source) own authority, reputation, inbound bank links, relevance, and anchor text. You cannot really impact this but you can ensure websites with poor reputation or spammy content either remove their links to you or you can use Google Webmaster tool to "Disavow" them (in other words "Disown" them). This means you declare to Google "Sorry, I did not ask for this link and please do not count it against me".

Good Link, Bad Link

Now you need to be aware of what is a bad link and which links are good. It is simple common sense, which means if someone charges you for a link, or the source website is full of links, or the website reputation is questionable, or the content is not relevant to your content, etc. you should avoid them. Also remember you cannot force people to remove their links to you, which is why Google has come up with the idea of "Disavow". Google used to ignore these links and did not pass any Link Juice to the target website, but in their wisdom they decided to make the website owner accountable! Welcome to crazy universe of Google.

Anchor Text

You may have noticed that some text (word or even entire sentence) in some websites are in different color and / or when you hover your mouse over them you see a link and if you click them you end up in another page or another website with content relevant to the highlighted text. This text is known as Anchor Text. You can see this in websites such as Wikipedia or our own website where you see text in Burgundy. The Anchor Text should ideally include keywords relevant to the target page content. This amplifies the value of the link.

Link Building

This is the process of actively searching out for websites to link to you. This can be done by directly contacting the right kind of websites (avoid directories) or by creating content including blogs that encourages people to link to your website page. Whatever you do, avoid paid links, swap links or get into triangular links where Website A links to Website B and Website B links to Website C and finally Website C links back to Website A. If the content of these websites are not relevant to you and they are seen as spam content or domain, they will harm you instead of help you.

Outbound Links

Now be aware that links from your website to other websites drain your "Link Juice" and pass some of it on to the target website. You may wish to do this as this may add value by encouraging the target website to link back to you. However, unless you see a real advantage in this you should use "No Follow" tag to signal to Google and other search engines to ignore this link. This is the same as "Disavow" but in reverse where you say to the Search Engine "Ignore this, I had to put this link here either for information only or I was forced for some reason but I am not giving them a vote or a boost or my Link Juice ".

Off Page SEO is an ongoing process which requires commitment, creativity, networking and a sprinkling of brilliance. Your job is never done. Even if you manage to get everything right and push all your competitors down to second place, it is unlikely that they will take it lying down and let you walk off with their lunch. Your competitors will fight back and try to reclaim their place, which sets off the entire cycle again.

Put these tactics and skills to work and you are sure to succeed. Keep in mind, consistency is key! You have to be consistent to reach goals or all they are is just dreams!

Graphics by Multiverse Design Co
@CoMultiverse

Essentials Only: A Success Guide to Self-Marketing

ABOUT THE AUTHOR

Baker started writing at a young age and become fascinated with marketing while trying to self-promote his first book. He dove in head-first and started learning everything he could about marketing. Now founder of his own marketing company, D. Baker Marketing, he couldn't be happier with what he does!

Website: https://dbakermarketing.com

Blog: https://www.dbakermarketing.com/blog

Twitter: @DBakerMarketing

Linkedin: https://www.linkedin.com/in/dustin-baker-983605201/

www.ingramcontent.com/pod-product-compliance
Lightning Source LLC
Chambersburg PA
CBHW071147240526
45465CB00024BA/1844